C000221805

Gallery Books
Editor Peter Fallon

HARBOUR LIGHTS

Derek Mahon

HARBOUR LIGHTS

Gallery Books

Harbour Lights
is first published
simultaneously in paperback
and in a clothbound edition
on 29 April 2005.

The Gallery Press
Loughcrew
Oldcastle
County Meath
Ireland

ISBN 1 85235 384 8 *paperback*
      1 85235 385 6 *clothbound*

A CIP catalogue record for this book
is available from the British Library.

Contents

for
Hugh and Fiona

PART ONE

Resistance Days

Nous nous aimerons tous et nos enfants riront
De la légende noire où pleure un solitaire.
— Paul Éluard

(*for John Minihan*)

The sort of snail-mail that can take a week
but suits my method, pre-*informatique*,
I write this from the St. Louis, rm. 14 —
or type it, rather, on the old machine,
a portable, that I take when I migrate
in 'the run-up to Christmas'. Here I sit
amidst the hubbub of the rue de Seine
while a winter fly snores at a window-pane.
Old existentialists, old beats, old punks
sat here of old; some dedicated drunks
still sing in the marketplace, and out the back
there's an old guy who knew Jack Kerouac.
Spring in December now, of course: no doubt
the daffs and daisies are already out
and you lot, in the serene post-Christmas lull,
biking the back roads between Hob and Schull.
Here at the *heure bleue* in the Deux Magots
where as a student I couldn't afford to go,
a gauche and unregenerate anglophone
tongue-tied as ever in my foreign tongue,
still getting the easiest constructions wrong,
I inhale the fashions of the sexy city,
its streets streaming with electricity,
its swings and roundabouts on the go as ever,
the fly-boats echoing on the floodlit river
when a switch locks and the long boulevard flares
with a thump and flow obscuring moon and stars.

In flight from corporate Christendom, this year
I spent the frightful season in Tangier
with spaced-out 'fiscal nomads' and ex-pats
or bored by Bowles beneath the sheltering slats,
bucket and spade under high cloud and sail,
blue and windblown, a sort of vast Kinsale
— a travel poster as we fluttered down
changing at Casablanca in pouring rain;
then ocean contours, minaret and souq,
a dribbling fountain, swirling palms, wind-sock,
a postcard; camels on the beach, black sheep
routinely scattering on the tiny strip,
the flowing script of Royal Air Maroc;
prescribed odours of cedarwood and kif
in the moist oasis of the Hotel du Rif,
swifts diving over the gardens and the port
of course, for even there the birds migrate;
heat-lightning flash photography in the strait,
eight lengths of a cold pool above a white
city at sea; keen carols on Christmas Day
with a lost tribe of Nigerian *sans-papiers,*
bright migrants from hot Sahara to cold EU
in the leafy English church Sam Beckett knew.

I'd uncles down that way in the war years,
a whole raft of Merchant Navy engineers,
northern barbarians on the Barbary Coast
in their white ducks, a far cry from Belfast —
old-movie time of transit visas, bad cheques,
the Dakar fiasco, 'everyone comes to Rick's';
but the proud Berbers of the west resist
the soul-stealing gaze of the 'western' tourist
to nurse the experience of a thousand years
beneath a crescent moon and evening stars
— al-'Dhara, al-'Debaran, al-Qa'id and al-Ta'ir —

peach-pink Arabian nights, the call to prayer
on Lavery's dunes and balconies, austere
as antelope or ibex, a light as rare:
you with your Nikon would go crazy there.

  A real barbarian, Wyndham Lewis, in flight
from daily mail, tube station and wireless set,
found there the desert 'blue' tribes he liked best
in the days of the Rif rifles and *Beau Geste,*
far from fake sheikhery and the coast hotels
exploring qasba art in the lunar hills —
'the best this side of China, I should say'.
Of course, most things are different since his day:
looking like Katie Tyrrell and the old folks
in your own 'sublimely gloomy' Athy pix,
as everywhere the filmable populations
have now been framed in shinier compositions,
the open prison of the corporate whole,
for even dissent has long been marketable —
even in the desert of legend and dark myth,
of drought and genocide, what Patti Smith
calls 'the real earth of Rimbaud', no daisies there.
Burroughs and Ginsberg — 9, rue Gît-le-Coeur —
who thought to undermine the monolith
were building new sandcastles in the air.

  Back now on the *rive gauche* and the Pont des Arts
re-reading the works of Bonnefoy and Éluard,
a *flâneur* in the dense galaxies of text
yet somehow knowing what to look for next,
I resist Miller's *Quiet Days in Clichy*
to browse among the picture books, *cliché*
and time exposure, the once bright machines,
the mirrored nudes like open nectarines,

high-definition fashion, *Paris de Nuit,*
copperplate silence, cranes at St. Denis,
the soap and tickets, the oblivious snow,
a gargoyle musing on the lights below,
soft-focus studio filter work, the glow
and heartening realism of Robert Doisneau
(industrial suburbs, the great aerial one
of the Renault plant beside the Bois de Boulogne,
pensioners, tramps, young lovers in a park,
a kiss at rush-hour or a dance in the dark);
and on the history shelves the wartime books,
old coats and bicycles, old hats and specs,
old sniper rifles, Gloria and Étoile
ripping up tarmac in the place St. Michel;
at the Gare du Nord a 24-hour clock,
clanking transports, faces wreathed in smoke
and the damned logo everywhere you look;
midnight editions, by Gironde or Loire
a distant grumble in the sky somewhere,
a shaky flashlight piercing night and cloud,
low voices murmuring like owls in a wood.
— Days of resistance, *un peu soviétique,*
plain Sartre and Beauvoir dancing cheek to cheek!

   Now our resistance is to co-optation,
the 'global' project of world domination,
the generative darkness hid from sight
in an earth strung with deterministic light
no more than a ganglion of wires and flex,
crap advertising and commercial sex.
Still sceptical, statistically off-line France
resists the specious arguments most advance,
the digital movies and unnatural nosh,
to stick with real tomatoes, real *brioche*
and real stars like Adjani and Binoche.

'No art without the resistance of the medium':
our own resistance to the murderous tedium
of business culture lays claim to the real
as product, no, but as its own ideal —
live seizures in the flux, fortuitous archetypes,
an art as fugitive as the life it snaps
tracing the magic of some primitive place
in the last retrenchment of the human face,
gossip and pigeons, close-ups by Kertész,
the young Diana in her London crèche.
Us snappers-up of photogenic details,
yourself a snapper of immortal souls,
resist commodity, the *ersatz*, the cold,
the *schrecklichkeit* of the post-modern world,
that the sun-writing of our resistance days
shine like Cape Clear glimpsed in a heat-haze.

After so much neglect, resolved anew,
creative anarchy I come back to you,
not the faux anarchy of media culture
but the real chaos of indifferent nature —
for instance, my own New Year resolution
is to study weather, clouds and their formation,
going straight to video with each new release
untroubled by the ignorant thought police.
I wish you good light or a light in a mist
safe from the critic and the invasive tourist,
a Munster twilight far from the venal roar
where waifs and strays can beat paths to your door,
unseasonal creatures, ears against the sky,
and timorous things that wouldn't hurt a fly,
conceptual silence, the best place to live —
'*Que faire d'une lampe, il pleut, le jour se lève*':
real daylight keeps on breaking, in other words.
So, love to Hammond and the karate kids;

down silent paths, in secret hiding places,
the locked out-house that no-one notices,
listening for footfalls by a quiet river
the sun will find us when the worst is over,
when everyone is in love, our children laugh
at the gruff bloke snuffling in the epigraph
and in the window-frame a persistent fly
buzzes with furious life which will never die.

PART TWO

Lucretius on Clouds

(*De Rerum Natura*, 6.451-523)

Clouds take shape in the blue sky and gather
where flying bodies get tangled up together;
tiny clouds are borne along by breezes
till the moment when a stronger current rises.
Hills, for instance: the higher up the peak
the more industriously they seem to smoke;
wind blows these wisps on to the mountain tops
while they are still vague, evanescent strips
and there, heaped up in greater quantity,
they reveal themselves as a visible entity
trailing from snowy summits into the ether,
the empyrean spaces torn by wind and weather.
Steam rises from the sea, as becomes clear
when clothes on the shore absorb the salty air;
particles rise from rivers and wet slopes
while the sky, weighing upon them, packs them tight
and weaves them closely like a linen sheet.
Some come from space, as I've explained before,
their number infinite, their source obscure,
and these can travel at the speed of light.
No wonder the storm clouds, so fast and thick,
darkening fields and sea, slide up so quick
since from the blow-holes of the outer spheres,
as in our own windpipes, our glands and pores
the elements come and go, mysterious and opaque,
through ducts and channels, rooms and corridors
as if in a house of opening, closing doors.
As for the rain clouds, how they come to grow
and fall as rain on the drinking earth below —
a multitude of life-germs, water semen, floats
with cloud stuff and secretions of all sorts,
both swollen up, the fat clouds and whatever
solution is in the clouds themselves, cloud-water,

as our own bodies grow with the serum, gism,
sweat, whatever fluid is in the organism;
also they draw up brine with streaming sieves
when wind drives the clouds over the waves,
hoisting it from the surface in dripping fleeces
(same thing with bogs and other soggy places).
When all these water-sources come together
clouds discharge their excess moisture either
by ganging up in a bunch to crush each other
till tears flow; or else, blown thin by winds
and sun-struck, they give off sizzling rains
as wax held to a brazier melts and runs.
Sometimes the two things coincide, of course,
the violent pushing and the rushing wind-force,
and then you get a cloudburst which persists
with clouds upon clouds, tempests upon tempests
pouring out of the heavens, soaking the smoky air
while the earth breathes back in bubbles everywhere.

High Water

Starved for pedestrian silence and in flight
from the 'totality and simultaneity' of data,
we stand on the Gesuati steps at high water
inhaling the rain-rinsed air of the Zattere.
Year-round tourism now, a perpetual high tide,
bright shadow of the present on old souls;
though still in a cool corner we can hide
with morning sunbeams at the swirling tiles,
a bracing sea-stench from the rotting piles,
hump bridges, monks and girls with parasols.
A paper moon dissolves in cloud canals,
the colours fading as they come to light.

Lapis Lazuli

(for Harry Clifton)

A whole night-sky that serves as a paperweight,
this azure block blown in from the universe
sits on my desk here, a still shimmering piece
of planet rock speckled with gold and white,
coarse-grained and knobbly as a meteorite
though recognized as a 'gem' in its own right.
The willow-pattern wisdom is still unknown,
the twinkling sages and the branchy house;
for this is the real thing in its natural state,
the raw material from which art is born.

Growth night-formed in sun-struck Afghanistan,
this complex chunk of sulphurous silicates
— a royal blue loved since the earth began
because, like the swirling sea, it never dates —
blinks authenticity through mysterious days
of slowly moving cloud and watery haze,
days of silence, watching as paint dries
while Buddha and a Yeats-head supervise.
Dim in the half-light of conventional rain,
we start at the squeal of Berkeley's telephone.

Slow fires still glowing in our cindery grates
even while the white, meridional sun vibrates
on sandy shelves where life first crept ashore,
we need the glitter of those secret depths
like the loved women of our private myths.
On dark dawns that look for that subtle gleam
and blinking noons obtuse to its dark dream
when slow thought replaces the money-shower,
we want the key to that impervious heart:
with ultramarine what need have we of art?

Heat lightning photographs the astonished sea.
Am I in Bermuda or in cold Sakhalin? Either
this new century with its bewildering weather
will work wonders for the sea-angling industry
or bring wolves dancing down the mooring ropes
of vast tankers and patronizing warships
to spill the bins and skate on the ice floes.
Do we die laughing or are we among those
for whom a spectre, some discredited ghost
still haunts the misty windows of old hopes?

While planes that consume deserts of gasoline
darken the sun in another rapacious war
a young woman reads alone in a lighted train,
scratches her scalp and shoves specs in her hair,
skipping the obvious for the rich and rare.
Hope lies with her as it always does really
and the twinkling sages in the Deux Magots
first glimpsed by a student forty years ago
on a continent like a plain of lapis lazuli;
and the Eurostar glides into the Gare du Nord.

Heathrow

Drugs, razors, cameras; *Lucozade replaces lost energy*, even in the strangest cases.

Hampstead Graves

The last resting-places at peace in mid-July —
white flash of cricket from a previous age
beyond the headstones and the boundary hedge.
Did Keats or Coleridge ever get down here?
Not open yet, and too far from the Heath.
Above the angels the planes shine and fly,
angels and insects; above willow, birch,
the modest outline of a local church,
some inscriptions buried by flower and leaf:
Mary-Anne, Miriam, Arthur, Jalal, Elizabeth
for ever in our hearts, who quit this life
… devoted father; dearly belovèd wife …
the Islamic sickle, simple as a scimitar,
the Celtic love-knot, the six-pointed star;
and the rear windows, blue suburban skies,
deckchair and brick, the penetrable mysteries.

'Things'

(for Jane)

It rained for years when I was young.
I sat there as in the old pop song
and stared at a lonely avenue
like everybody else I knew
until, one day, the sun came out.
I too came out, to shout and sing
and see what it was all about.
Oh yes, I remember everything.

The Cloud Ceiling

An ocean-drop, dash in the dark, flash in the brain,
suspension in the red mist, in the light-grain,
a twitching silence in the hiding place,
fine pearly night-glow of the forming face,
the pushing brow, the twirling ears and knees ...
Space-girl, soap on a rope, you like cloud-swing,
bath-water and world music; a kidney-bean,
you lie there dreaming on your knotted string
listening hard with shut, determined eyes —
a soul of barely determinate shape and size.

Are thoughts a tap trickle, a cloud formation?
Given to light readings and rich inactivity,
alternative galaxies, a-tonal composition
and tentative revisions of quantum gravity,
you drift in a universe of unspoken words
far from the bright lights and story-boards.
A shy girl in your own private microcosm,
you travel from cloud-chasm to cloud-chasm
awaiting the moment when the burbles start,
the camera action, the first signs of art;

and enter like one of Aristophanes' cloud chorus
heard 'singing in the distance' though not for us,
daughters of ocean for whom alone we write,
grave sisters of the rainbow, rose and iris
who dip their pitchers in the sea at night
and soak the risen leaf before first light —
capricious dirigibles of the swirling ether,
great wringing sacks above the luminous earth
from whose precipitations images gather
as in the opacity of a developing-bath.

After a night of iron-dark, unmoving skies
you open your eyes; we too open our eyes
on a clear day where hedgerow and high-rise
swivel deliriously round your baby-bed
in the attic studio where you lie safe
like yin and yang in your own secret life.
Sunlight streams like April at the window;
sky-flocks graze above your dreaming head.
Life is a dream, of course, as we all know,
but one to be dreamt in earnest even so.

We've painted a cloud ceiling, a splash of stars
and a thin convective stream, not a bad job:
'Who can number the clouds in wisdom?' (Job).
The indeterminate firmament is all yours.
Rain glitters along a branch, the earth revolves;
soft toys stare, wide-eyed, from the bookshelves.
Will you be Echo, Gráinne, Rosalind? No,
you won't be any of these; you will be you
as, 'kitten-soft', you float from the mother ship,
thirst pockets open for the infinite trip.

I who, though soft-hearted, always admired
granite and blackthorn and the verse hard-wired,
tingle and flow like January thaw-water
in contemplation of this rosy daughter.
Be patient with an old bloke; remember later
one who, in his own strange, distracted youth
awake to the cold stars for the harsh truth,
now tilts a bottle to your open mouth.
So drench the nappies; fluff, bubble and burp:
I probably won't be here when you've grown up.

During the War

There are those of us who say 'during the war'
as if the insane scramble for global power
doesn't continue much as it did before.
Red buses and black taxis then as now
in thundering London, even in sloppy Soho.
The light-bowl flickers and the lifts are slow
but I bounce on sneakers up a winding stair:
even at sixty I can still walk on air.

I'm reading Bowen again in mysterious Kôr
and picturing the black-out in Regent's Park,
fierce moonlight blazing down on rail and door,
lost lovers, changing lights, fugitive smiles,
one car, silence, ponds white in the dark,
the whole place clearly visible for miles —
now visible, a bright smudge, from outer space.
No serious myth since the first days of 'peace'.

...This morning in Wardour St., a skip, a tip,
a broken pipe, some unfinished repair work.
A basin of mud and junk has choked it up,
reflecting the blown sky and a baroque
cloud cinema beyond earthly intercourse:
a hole in the road where cloud-leaves gather,
each one framed for a moment in stagnant water
and trailing out of the picture in due course.

This is nothing, this is the triumph of time,
waste products mixing in the history bin,
rain ringing with a harsh, deliberate chime
on scrap iron, plastic and depleted tin,
its grim persistence from the rush-hour sky
a nuisance to the retail trade. Andrei
on his back, wounded, during his own war:
'I never really saw the clouds before ...'

No more shy whispers in a darkening square.
Strip lighting writes the dusk out everywhere
on corporate space and stadium, while slow
flashes go hacking up like tracer fire
and lasers fence among the clouds for show.
The spiteful rain, filmic, begins to freeze,
grown sentimental and considering snow:
to spin at leisure amid naked trees!

December night; night vision; a slash of hail.
An east wind gathering force on water streams
up here like shirts blown from the shining Thames
to *Ronnie Scott's* and *Mme. JoJo's, Soho Jazz & Soul.*
Time now to watch for the dawn of a new age.
Down there, gleaming amid the porn and veg.,
its rippling skin mutating by the minute,
a shivering dump with one faint star in it.

Langue d'Oc

(*Guilhem IX d'Aquitaine, 12th c.*)

1

At the first warmth of spring
the forest fills with leaves;
each bird in its own tongue
whistles a new tune:
time now to look again
at our own lives and loves.

2

She sends no word of hope
to set my heart at ease.
I neither laugh nor sleep
nor can I concentrate,
not knowing if the upshot
will be the one I choose.

3

Our love is a hawthorn branch
shaking at night against
a sky of wind and rain
until the rising sun
spreads itself and glows
among the leaves and boughs.

4

One morning sticks in the mind:
while we lay dim and fond
she made me the gift of her
intimacy and fervour.
Soon may my busy hand
be in her skirt for ever.

5

Cheap rumours left and right
threaten our fierce desire
and force us far apart.
Danger, what do we care?
No malice, no envious spite
can spoil the thing we share.

A Game of Cards

(*Tadhg Ó Ruairc, 17th c.*)

*At the time card games like 'tables' often figured as
erotic confrontations. Blánaid is otherwise unknown.*

Blánaid, I face you, gorgeous foe,
   girl of the wavy gold chevelure,
each curl long and provocative
   reaching down to the forest floor.

Crazy about you, as you know,
   your grey eyes and lingering looks,
your round cheeks where roses glow,
   the eyebrows like two pen-strokes,

I listen to the languorous voice
   where your superior nature sings,
a finer sound than organ pipe
   or lute, sweeter than harp-strings,

and dote upon your skilful hands,
   the long fingers and pink nails
designed to pluck a tremulous note
   or draw ink from quivering quills;

the perfect opalescent breast
   no knight or knave has ever known,
the slender body and slim waist:
   Blánaid, I play for you alone.

The game is up if I should glimpse
   a flash of knee or open side,
white ankle-flicker, pale instep,
   toes creamy as the incoming tide;

but take me with a daring move,
    bright woman of the devious mind.
Be generous with your secret love,
    relieve me of my dubious hand.

It beats me you can keep in check
    a rogue like me so quick to sin.
Strip poker, scrabble, snap, bezique:
    whatever the game, we both can win.

So put your cards on the table, dear;
    shuffle the deck and shake the dice.
It's serious stakes we play for here
    and high time you showed your ace!

Jean Rhys in Kettner's

1

I'm crouching here in the corner, a kind of ghost
but safe with my Craven 'A' and Gordon's gin,
wearing a cloche hat and an old fox fur
and skimming *Vogue* with my distracted air.
The rush-hour crowd a hail-storm ushers in
heaves at the bar like flotsam in flat seas
(I looked it up: *sargaço*, n., Portuguese)
and scares me slightly in the window seat
where I shiver, no doubt looking a bit lost
remembering cane fields in Dominican heat,
a gone-with-the-windward isle of the unblest,
the harsh plantations and the dark voyage
— somewhere I lived once in another age
with thunder, magic and the scent of jasmine.

2

Not easy to be a woman in the old world —
the quick presumption, the frank stare as though
one achieved little on this earth, at least
little of what the wise world calls achieving.
Reader, I was a tedious, nightmare guest
who never learned the common art of living
but died triumphant and amazed at how
the secrecies I harboured as a child,
under the skin, were recognized at last.
'Writing I don't know; other things I know':
what children now in the gardens of Roseau?
Blown there by the discredited trade-winds,
bewitched, bewildered, in at least two minds,
we found no true home in our chosen west.

3

The pianist plays show numbers and thirties jazz.
A slave in my turn, one to be bought and sold,
once hot and anxious, then aghast and cold,
I'd come here with the other chorus girls,
each in a short skirt and a string of pearls,
and men whose eyes were an anonymous glaze.
A life of boarding houses and cheap hotels
and I snag like a blown bag in a thorn-field
snapping and scratching, fighting to keep sane
in a new age; and so the soul survives.
Released at last, I lived out my two lives
between the water and the *vie en rose*:
the bottles ting-a-ling between hedgerows,
a draughty house at the end of a country lane.

PART THREE

The Widow of Kinsale

Cionn tSáile, 'Head of the Tide',
knew me once as a young bride
but those days are gone;
a rock exposed to the sun,
sardonic, cold and stiff,
I go with the ebb of life.

The salt surge in my veins
whispers its age and drains
down to the shrinking sea:
no more high tide for me.
Stylish I was and not
got up in this old coat.

Young ones now think only
of fashion and easy money —
as we did once, except
we never had much of it:
real people were the thing,
to hear them talk and sing.

When I was a girl we thought
more highly of our admirers.
I opened my young body
gravely to their desires;
now I am an old lady,
unwanted and unsought.

War widow and sea widow
many years on the shelf,
I'm hardly even a shadow
of my once sexy self,
my beauty and high tone
nothing but skin and bone.

I was a fierce temptation
to wild, generous men
of my own generation;
lovingly I would watch
while driving them insane.
Now look at this eyepatch.

Once a wife and mother
beset by childish squabbles,
I live alone with a plethora
of stuff in the loud fridge:
plaice, chops and vegetables,
enough for a new ice age.

I who was bright and gay
in the wine-and-roses years
am briskly polite today
to gossipy old neighbours;
my white head in the clouds,
I avoid the holiday crowds.

Crows croak from the convent
where once we used to skip.
Everything has been taken
since it is not convenient;
the upper windows are broken,
the lower ones boarded up.

Sometimes I drive over
in my old-fashioned Rover
to Bantry or even Dingle
and think of the times I knew
when everyone was single;
but now they are so few

that mostly I prefer
a comfortable armchair.
I could re-read for ever
the novels of William Trevor,
that lovely man, and watch
starlight in the dark porch.

Calm and alone at last,
I wake up in the night.
A superstitious atheist,
I now befriend the clergy
and go to church despite
the new revised liturgy;

but my true guiding spirit
is something I inherit,
a thing dim and opaque,
a lighthouse in the fog,
a lamp hung in a wood
to light my solitude,

breastplate and consolation
whatever the situation:
increasing aches and pains,
the silence in the womb
as the life-force wanes,
my children far from home.

The best place is the strand,
its primitive life-forms
when the last light warms
islands of shining sand
and the ebb-tide withdraws
with a chuckle of bony claws.

A Garden God

A bomber fly flits from the ruined mouth;
from the eye-socket an inquisitive moth.

The Enchanted Wood

(after Valéry)

Amid rustling leaves and leaf-shadows her moist
breath rises and falls in the silent hall;
magpies alight beside her glittering wrist,
her lips almost compose one coral vowel.
She listens neither to the quiet raindrops
tinkling the coin of the submerged decades
nor to the flute-wind in the dreaming copse
where the horn-note of a distant hunt subsides.

To these dwindling echoes she faintly sighs,
grown indistinct among the light brambles
waving and tapping at her buried ear;
and the slow rose whispering to her eyes
never discountenances the warm dimples
secretly conscious of the sunlight there.

Bashō in Kinsale

Samurai cries from
Enthusiasts in the gym
As I wander home.

Dithery rain-lines;
Crows glisten in the branches
Of listening pines.

Gulls in the clear air,
Hawthorn snow in the hedges;
Soon you will be here.

March, evening shadow
On pine and quiet dockyard
Here in Hokkaido.

Clouds obscure the night
Giving our eyes a rest from
The intense moonlight.

Rough sea after dark;
Blazing over the harbour
The fierce zodiac.

A heron voice harsh
Above us after midnight
Like a lightning-flash.

Walking each evening
At a slower pace, we hear
The dark river sing.

A morning of mist;
No light-source but a hidden
Sun burns in the east.

A cove, flies and fleas,
Wrack magic in salt sea-air
And the faintest breeze.

These old childish things,
Big blisters at the shoreline,
Are my water wings.

Blown sand and no talk,
Even the most northern road
An easier walk.

Desert island books:
Homer and Rachel Carson,
Durable hardbacks.

Sketch of a sail race,
The work of many summers:
A few lines in space.

Shorelines

*This sequence is based on a series of photographs
by the Cork artist Vivienne Roche.*

Driftwood and cloud castle,
expiring lines of froth,
absorbing sand where every
worm-hole is a discovery:
two worlds, earth and air;
water, the best of both.

Breakwater, an ebbing tide,
the frantic shingle-dash
and vigilant gull-glide,
cold eyes on whatever blind
nourishment the wave-wash,
receding, leaves behind.

These sand studies, these
vitreous transparencies
expose each bare feature:
original rock sculpture,
rubble and ropes of cream
as graphic as any dream.

This one, taken at night
or nearly, shows a flight
of clustering sun-splinters,
a rippling archipelago
of silvery star cinders
the light left long ago.

There is a special calm
in the rising sea-level;
quietude, cool but warm,
the surface a hushed veil
where you expect a fin
or a spinning dolphin.

Closer in, slipping aside
from the furious tide-race,
a swirl of incoming tide
has signed a separate peace
with sighs and whisperings,
its ripples silent strings,

each one a thoughtful stave
next to the bath-house roar,
air garden and wind bower
where each slow-motion wave
is a blue note designed
to calm the riotous mind —

proposing, like a soul breeze
or random natural noise,
a new kind of 'found'
spirit-breathing music:
not pop, please, but the basic
tones of an ancient sound.

Resistant, a losing struggle,
the breakwater descends
from quick-shelving sands;
seaward the stanchions stride
into the roar and giggle
of a punctual high tide.

The long contingent action
of salt on the first rocks,
a never ceasing friction,
no respite and no pity:
this is the raw reality,
always that harsh index.

Wrack whips whistle and snore,
then near-silence once more
as the tide reconsiders;
rough face of the waters.
But flick of a wren-wing
and she sits on a rock to sing.

Where to Hide

(Some derelict beach hut or abandoned wreck
as in that strange novel by Yann Queffélec.)

New Wave

On the first day of principal photography
they sit outside at a St. Germain café
with coffee cups between them on a round
table of chequered oilcloth red and grey.
The hand-held camera looks for natural light,
mikes pick up traffic and incidental sound.
A mid-week noon and the hot bridges sweat;
from ice buckets, from windows, watches, knives,
life flashes back at them their glittering lives.

Silence, the first thing they have in common,
creates a little precise hole in the uproar
and the vague sorrow between man and woman
changes summer to autumn as they conspire
like scientists working from the same data.
When they reach Cabourg beyond a darkening road
and a white hotel room shaken by white waves
in a cloud of powder and brine, they run baths
and stare at the moon through open windows.

While the lamps go off along the promenade
they wake to a dawn silence, curtained light,
mist and roar of the sea, vast dazzling cloud;
but the stripped mind, still moist and nocturnal,
flinches from confrontation with the infinite.
The sky, its racing stripes and ice-cream colours,
thin cries of children from the beach below,
and the hurtling gulls, are too heartbreaking;
they shut the shutters and return to the dark.

They live the hours as others live the years.
A plane sky-writes, sails flock on the horizon,
their sheets stretch to the white lines of surf
and they doze as if on their own patch of sand
with wind and sun combing their backs and thighs

in a dream of dune-light and rustling quartz
worn smooth by night winds since the dawn of time.
Air reigns, mother-of-pearl; flies come and go;
they open and close their fists like the newly born.

He has given up even on the death of language
and a shower of dots relieves his final page ...
A singer, tonight she sings in the casino
to a shiny ring of bourgeois, but her heart
has already taken flight from the car-park.
Tide-click; starry wavelengths; aquarium light
from the old world picks out in a double row
their sandy prints where, orphans going home,
they climb back into the waves in a snow of foam.

Red Cloud

(after Bonnefoy)

I used to play in the back garden at first
Watching the spring sky for an end to war,
But clouds came up and the wind dispersed
My futile phrases with a dazzling roar.

We used to make love in an open meadow
But a wild electric energy would stir
Between two towering banks of shadow
Till finally, in a trembling of the air,

We stared at unknown countries, shining weather,
Unvisited seas beyond, celestial roads,
Dim thunder grumbling elsewhere in the ether
As if to appease the elemental gods.

Above the windblown lovers where they murmur,
The child at its amusements, an unbroken
Cloud series rimmed with ecliptic glimmer
Which lingers there this evening like a token.

White Cloud

(*after Brecht*)

One evening in the blue month of September
We lay at peace beneath an apple bough.
I took her in my arms, my gentle lover,
And held her closely like a dream come true —
While far up in the tranquil summer heaven
There was a cloud, I saw it high and clear;
It was so white and so immense above us
And, as I watched, it was no longer there.

Since then so very many different evenings
Have drifted blindly past in the general flow;
Perhaps the apple orchards have been flattened,
And if you ask me where the girl is now
I have to admit I really don't remember.
I can imagine what you're going to say
But even her face I truly can't recapture,
I only know I kissed it there that day.

Even the kiss I would have long forgotten
If that one cloud had not been up there too —
I see it and will always see it plainly,
So white and unexpected in the blue.
Perhaps the apple boughs are back in blossom,
Maybe she holds a fourth child on her knees;
The cloud, though, hung there for a moment only
And, as I watched, it broke up in the breeze.

On the Beach

1

You want a serene old age?
Cold front and icy ridge,
briny bubble and squeak
and the tributary leak
are waiting for you here;
flea-wrack, a stench of tar —

2

and the ancient art of leisure
best practised not on any
petrol-blue *côte d'azur*
with its bums and money
but in the fresh exposure
of a single sea-anemone.

Calypso

Homer was wrong, she never 'ceased to please'.
Once he'd escaped from Circe's magic castle,
the toxic bowl, shape-shifting witcheries;
from the underworld, from Aeolus' watery roar,
the high-pitched Sirens' penetrating whistle,
cliff monsters, divine anger, broken boats,
on soft, tinkling shingle he crept ashore
through juniper and parsley, cows and goats,
and found the hot path to her open door,
a cart parked in the lane, a smoking fire.

Gaily distracting him from his chief design
she welcomed him with open arms and thighs,
teaching alternatives to war and power.
A wild girl rushing to the head like wine,
she held him closely with her braided coils,
her swift insistence, aromatic oils,
her mild, beguiling glance, tuning his days
to a slow sea-rhythm; and through a salty haze
he watched her moving as in a golden shower
or swimming with her nymphs from the sea-shore.

Red sails in the sunset where the dripping prows
rapped out a drum-rhythm on uncertain seas
of skimming birds, a lonely pine or shrine —
but the sea's secrets diminished on dry land,
darker than they could know or understand,
and vanished in a blink, night coming on
wherever they put ashore to rest. A whorled
conch whispered about a recent, far-off world
with oars sunk in sand marking the graves
of those lost to chance or vindictive waves.

Some harsh, some murderous with savage gulls
squatting in triumph amid scattered skulls
buzzing with flies, he knew unfortunate isles,
the eternal conflict between sea and stone,
the palpitating heat of the noon sun.
He prayed for an end to these moronic wars,
burned wasteful sacrifices to the vague stars
and dreamed of honey, yoghurt, figs and wine
on night beaches far from the life he knew,
silent, unlit; but a faint murmur, a faint glow.

Those were the times he thought about his wife,
remembering their lives in a former life,
her handsome profile, her adventurous heart
and proud demeanour. At sea and lost he wept
for jokes and music, promises unkept,
sandals on board and tile, shared places, friends,
shared history, origins, those woods and glens,
his brisk departure from the family hearth
a glib mistake; but nature took its course
leaving him desolation and long remorse.

Ithaca, 'home', not far now as the kite flew,
he sniffed those evenings when a sea-wind blew
but lingered in that cool cave behind the dunes
enchanted now by hazel and sea-grey eyes,
the star-flow of the hair, the skittish tones,
sand-quivering foam, long leisure, lip and gland
in the early-morning light, the sun ablaze
through leaves and linen, through her open hand,
briar and cumuli; so the years unwound
to a whisper of spring water and kitchen noise.

Homer was right though about the important thing,
the redemptive power of women; for this narrative,
unlike the blinding shields, is womanly stuff.
The witch bewitches, the owl-winged sisters sing,
some kind girl takes charge within the shadow
of a calm glade where the sea finds a meadow;
much-sought Penelope in her new resolute life
has wasted no time acting the stricken widow
and even the face that sank the final skiff
knows more than beauty; beauty is not enough.

Penelope, of course, with the husband gone,
was instantly besieged by plausible men
and the wild rumours now in circulation;
the palace, ruined by competing suitors,
hosted intrigue, conspiracy and confusion,
its shadow crumbling in Ionian waters.
He knew nothing of this; or, if he did,
felt he had no more heart now for a fight,
asking the Pleiades or a drifting cloud
to let these things unravel as best they might.

He spent his days there in a perpetual summer.
Stuck in a rock-cleft like a beachcomber
washed up, high and dry amid luminous spray,
intent on pond life, wildflowers and wind-play,
the immense significance of a skittering ant,
a dolphin-leap or a plunging cormorant,
he learned to live at peace with violent nature,
calm under the skies' grumbling cloud-furniture
and bored by practical tackle, iron and grease —
an ex-king and the first philosopher in Greece.

Bemused with his straw hat and driftwood stick,
unmoved by the new wars and the new ships,
he died there, fame and vigour in eclipse,
listening to voices echo, decks and crates
creak in the harbour like tectonic plates —
or was he sharp still in his blithe disgrace,
deliberate pilot of his own foggy shipwreck?
Homer was wrong, he never made it back; or,
if he did, spent many a curious night hour
still questioning that strange, oracular face.

Harbour Lights

And I...a mere newcomer whose ancestors had
inhabited the earth so briefly that my presence was
almost anachronistic.
          — Rachel Carson, *The Edge of the Sea*

It's one more sedative evening in Co. Cork.
The house is quiet and the world is dark
while the Bush gang are doing it to Iraq.
The flesh is weary and I've read the books;
nothing but lies and nonsense on the box
whose light-dot vanishes with a short whine
leaving only a grey ghost in the machine.
Slick boats click at the quayside down below
the drowsy bungalows of the well-to-do;
late light illuminates the closing pub,
shop window, leisure centre and sailing club,
exhausted cars tucked up in their garages,
rabbits and foxes, birds dumb in the hedges;
midsummer light shifting its general blaze
sets in a secret thicket of hazel trees,
on garden sheds and lined pre-Cambrian rock
red as the wavy roof-tiles of Languedoc.
Re-reading history page by lamplit page,
imagining the lost poems of Iníon Dubh,
I could be living here in another age
except at week-ends when the bikes converge.
Blow-in asylum and dormitory of privilege,
its dreamy woods are straight out of Chekhov,
quaint gardens made for 19th-century love;
trans-national, the skies are Indian skies,
the harbour lights Chinese or Japanese;
and certain thatchy corners the gull sees
keep the last traces of the bardic phase,
straw spaces echoing to disconsolate cries.

Get out more? I prefer to watch by starlight
the London plane, a galaxy in flight,
night-shining cloud, a ghost ship among stars,
and the light fading from our western shores.
It's now that the high spirits begin to drop,
remembering buried errors and wasted time;
but in the morning when the sun comes up
there will be snail-mail with its pearly gleam
and a gruff husky scratching on the gravel,
young people chattering as in a Russian novel,
sky-shining roofs where smoky notions rise,
back yards where the drainpipes soliloquize,
a wood-shriek as a whining saw spins free
and the wild soul flies from a stricken tree.
Alive to voices and, to my own surprise,
up with the lark, up with the June sunrise,
I study the visible lines of tidal flow,
the spidery leaves alight with sweat and dew,
doors blazing primary colours, blue and red,
phone-lines at angles against bundling cloud.

Go wandering with your stick on the back road,
you start with a ruined convent school, a tough
chough cursing you from a lichen-speckled roof;
organic fields to the left; and, to the right,
the mud basin of one more building site.
Startling how fast a thing can integrate:
beneath those tiles some immigrant teenager
will write the unknown poetry of the future.
Sun-ripples on the trout-shimmering Bandon River
where on a clear day you can see for ever;
a flash of foam like Gray's *Great Wave at Sète*,
alternate light and shade on the shut eyes,
the untaken photograph and the unwritten phrase;
woof of a terrier, crash of a fluttering wing,

the bird-voiced tinkle of a hidden spring.
Now, note that white sail where a dinghy moves,
a raw strand where Cúchulainn fought the waves,
a writhing Daphne thorn-tree, hands and hair
mute but articulate in the Atlantic air,
chained in the ivy strings that bind her there
while somebody takes shape in the heat haze:
a young woman in track-suit and running shoes.
A cloud covers the sun and a quick shower
scribbles with many pencils on the estuary,
the coves, the beaches and the open sea,
sub-tropical wave-light where it calmly roars
at dark soul-cottages with their shining doors,
the docks in fierce, eye-straining definition,
each thing distinct but in oblique relation;
the faux schooner bearing a famous name,
a pocket cruise-ship like a video game.

   Back at the house revisit the dark grove
of baths, old cars and fridges, while above
a withered orchard the slow cloud-cranes move
in the empty silence where a myth might start
— flute-note, god-word — the first whisper of art
withdrawn in its integrity, in its own
obscurity, for not everything need be known.
Magic survives only where blind profit,
so quick on the uptake, takes no notice of it
for ours is a crude culture dazed with money,
a flighty future that would ditch its granny.
The orchard withers but the birds sing on
through the long morning, and in the afternoon
you watch clouds gather and disperse, paint dry,
and listen patiently to the wasp and fly.

But everything is noticed, everything known
in the 'knowledge era', advertised as the one
without precedent; though in late middle age,
striving to tame the Yeatsian lust and rage,
I claim the now disgraceful privilege
of living part-time in a subversive past:
'... fall and are built again'; nor is this the last,
for the tough nuts, imagining you fortunate,
will aim to get you with their curious hate.
Try the Blue Haven, its interior bright
with port-holes and chronometers, spare parts;
winking in turn, a frieze of lighthouse charts.

Lady, whose shrine stands on the promontory
above the fancy golf-course, taking inventory
of vapour trails and nuclear submarines,
keep close watch on our flight paths and sea-lanes,
our tourist coaches and our slot machines,
the cash dynamic and the natural gas.
Your arbour stands there as it always has,
secret and shy above these baffling shores
and the white-winged oceanic water table.
A short path and a tumbler of fresh flowers,
a cup of dusty water, bead and pebble,
the salt-whipped plaster of your serious head,
an azure radiance in your tiny shed
gazing out over the transatlantic cable
with a chipped eye towards Galicia and the Azores.

I toy with cloud thoughts as an alternative
to the global shit-storm that we know and love,
but unsustainable levels of aviation
have complicated this vague resolution;
for even clouds are gobbled up by the sun,
not even the ethereal clouds are quite immune:

these too will be marketed if it can be done.
I was here once before, though, at Kinsale
with the mad chiefs, and lived to tell the tale;
I too froze in the hills, first of the name
in Monaghan, great my pride and great my shame —
or was it a slander that we tipped them off,
old Hugh asking a quart of Power's from Taaffe?
Does it matter now? Oh yes, it still matters;
strange currents circulate in these calm waters
though we don't mention them, we talk instead
of the new golf-course out at the Old Head.
What have I achieved? Oh, little enough, God knows:
some dubious verse and some ephemeral prose;
as for the re-enchantment of the sky,
that option was never really going to fly
but it's too late to do much about it now
except to trust in the contumacious few
who aren't afraid to point to an obvious truth,
and the frank stare of unpredictable youth.

    A buoy nods faintly in the harbour mouth
as I slope down to the front for a last walk
and watch trawlers disgorging at the dock
in the loud work-glow of a Romanian freighter,
dark oil-drums and fish boxes on the quay,
winches and ropes, intestines of the sea
alive with the stench of pre-historic water.
I've noted codgers, when the day is done,
sitting in easy rows in the evening sun
before the plate-faced rising moon creates
a sphere of influence where thought incubates
with midnight oil and those old harbour lights,
'the harbour lights that once brought you to me'.
White page, dark world; wave theory; moon and pines:
thin as an aspirin that vast surface shines,

the pits and heights in intimate close-up,
her bowed head grave as through a telescope
as if aware of danger; for quite soon,
perhaps, we dump our rubbish on the moon.
The new dark ages have been fiercely lit
to banish shadow and the difficult spirit;
yet here, an hour from the night-shining city
ablaze with its own structural electricity,
sporadic pinpoints star the archaic night
older and clearer than any glow we generate.

    Outside the exhausted kids have wandered home;
the house is quiet, calm till the next storm:
when the time comes and if the coast is clear,
work in some sort of order, let me hear
the cries of children playing but not too near.
Tick of real time, the dark realities
in the unreality of the mental gaze;
a watery murmur, a drip of diesel oil,
night silence listening to the dozy soul,
the waves' confusion in the void. 'No dice',
said Einstein; but each bit of rock might claim
a different origin if it took its time,
the faintest starfish with its pointed wobble
might tell us otherwise if it took the trouble
and even the tiniest night-rustling pebble
might solve the mystery if it had a voice;
for everything is water, the world a wave,
whole populations quietly on the move.

    Will the long voyage end here among friends
and swimming with a loved one from white strands,
the sea loud in our veins? It never ends
or ends before we know it, for everyone
'stands at the heart of life, pierced by the sun,

and suddenly it's evening' (Quasimodo);
suddenly we're throwing a longer shadow.
The hermit crab crawls to its holiday home;
dim souls wriggle in seething chaos, body
language and new thought forming there already
in hidden depths and exposed rock oases,
those secret cultures where the sky pauses,
sand flats, a whispery fringe discharging gases,
a white dish drained by the receding sea
and trailing runic whips of tangled hair
brushed and combed by the tide, exhaling air.
No, this is Galápagos and the old life-force
rides Daz and Exxon to the blinding surface.
Down there a drenching of the wilful sperm,
congenital sea-fight of the shrimp and worm
with somewhere the soft impulse of a lover,
the millions swarming into pond and river
to find the right place, find it and live for ever ... ?

PART FOUR

The Seaside Cemetery

(after Valéry)

Inspired by the Mont St. Clair cemetery in Paul Valéry's home town of Sète, south-west France, 'Le Cimetière marin' was begun in July, 1917, and first published in 1920.

A tranquil surface where a spinnaker moves
flickers among the pines, among the graves;
objective noon films with its fiery glaze
a shifting sea, drifters like dipping doves,
and my reward for thought is a long gaze
down the blue silence of celestial groves.

When, as now, light freezes above the gulf,
a gem revolving in its radiant gleam
such many-faceted and glittering foam
that a great peace seems to extend itself,
those clear-cut artifacts of the continuum,
time and knowledge, take the shape of a dream.

Wide-open vault and chaste shrine to Athene,
deep reservoir of calmly shining money,
like an eye the supercilious water structure
lies somnolent beneath its burning veils;
and my soul-silence too is architecture,
a golden hoard roofed with a thousand tiles.

Temple of time I breathe when I breathe in,
to this high point I climb and feel at home
ordering all things with a seaward stare
of circumspection; and, as my supreme
offering to the gods, the serene glare
sows on the depths an imperious disdain.

But even as fruit consumes itself in taste,
even as it translates its own demise
deliciously in the mouth where its form dies,
I sniff already my own future smoke
while light sings to the ashen soul the quick
change starting now on the murmuring coast.

Under this clear sky it is I who change —
after so much conceit, after such strange
decadence, but bursting with new power,
I give myself up to these brilliant spaces;
on the mansions of the dead my shadow passes
reminding me of its own ephemeral hour.

A soul-exposure to the solar torches
I can endure, and the condign tortures
of the midsummer's pitiless bronze light;
and though submission show a midnight face
invisible in daytime, to that bright
presence I concede the superior place.

Stopped at a cistern with a pumping heart
between the vacuum and the creative act
whispering to my preliminary tact,
I await the echo of an interior force,
that bitter, dark and sonorous water-source
ringing in depths beyond the reach of art.

Caged though you seem behind a mesh of branches,
great gulf, consumer of these meagre fences,
a blinding secret on the lids, reveal
what body draws me to its indolences,
what face invites me to this bony soil.
A faint spark ponders these inheritances.

Composed of sombre trees, of light and stone,
an earthly splinter held up to the sun,
sacred, enclosed in immaterial fire,
I like this place with its dark poplar flames,
the marble glimmering in the shadows here
where a faithful sea snores on the table-tombs.

And if, sole shepherd, with a pastoral eye
I gaze too long on these mysterious flocks,
on these white souls, each in its tranquil box,
may the sea's growl dispel the idolatrous things,
frightening off the prudent doves, the coy
illusions and the angels' curious wings.

The future, here already, scarcely moves.
A quick insect scratches the dry leaves;
everything is exhausted, scorched by the air
into I don't know what rigorous form.
Dazed with diversity, the enormous swarm
of life is bitter-sweet and the mind clear.

The hidden dead lie easy in this soil
which holds them tight and seasons their mystique;
high up the southern noon, completely still,
reflects upon itself where none may look.
Absolute monarch, firmament of blue,
I am the secret difference now in you.

I am the one your worst fears validate —
my cowardice, my bad thoughts, my contrition
make up the one flaw in your precious opal;
and meanwhile, in a dense marmoreal night
among the roots, vague oceanic people
have long ago arrived at your conclusion.

Mixed in a thick solution underground
the white clay is drunk by the crimson kind;
its vigour circulates in the veined flowers.
Where now are the colloquial turns of phrase,
the individual gifts and singular souls?
Where once a tear gathered the grub crawls.

The ticklish virgins with their twittering cries,
the teeth, the eyelids and the gentle eyes,
enchanted breasts heaving in provocation,
glistening lips shiny with invitation,
the last delights, the fingers that resist,
all join the circle and return to dust.

And you, great soul, dare you hypostasize
a world untarnished by the luminous lies
the sun and sea suggest to mortal eyes?
Will you still sing when you've become a ghost?
Nonsense, everything flows, ourselves the most;
the hunger for eternity also dies.

Gaunt immortality, gold carved on black,
cold consolation crowned with a laurel wreath
that makes a maternal bosom of grim death,
a gorgeous fiction and a lugubrious joke —
who doesn't know, and who would not decline
the empty skull with its eternal grin?

Archaic progenitors, your derelict heads
returned to pasture by so many spades,
no longer knowing the familiar tread —
the real ravager, the irrefutable worm
is not for you, at peace now in the tomb;
it lives on life and never leaves my side.

Self-love, self-hatred, what's the difference?
Its secret mordancy is so intense
the silent gnawing goes by many names.
Watching, desiring, nibbling, considering,
it likes the flesh and, even in my dreams,
I live on sufferance of this ravenous thing.

Zeno, harsh theorist of conceptual zero,
have you transfixed me with your winged arrow
which quivers, flies, yet doesn't fly at all?
Does the twang wake me and the arrow kill?
Sunlight, is it merely a tortoise-shade,
the mighty hero frozen in mid-stride?

No, no; get up; go on to the next phase —
body, shake off this meditative pose
and, chest, inhale the first flap of the air.
A palpable new freshness off the sea,
an ozone rush, restores my soul to me
and draws me down to the reviving shore.

Great sea endowed with frenzy and sensation,
slick panther-hide and heaving vegetation
sown with a million images of the sun;
unchained monster drunk on your blue skin,
chewing for ever your own glistening tail
in a perpetual, silent-seeming turmoil,

the wind rises; it's time to start. A vast breeze
opens and shuts the notebook on my knees
and powdery waves explode among the rocks
flashing; fly off, then, my sun-dazzled pages
and break, waves, break up with ecstatic surges
this shifting surface where the spinnaker flocks!

Acknowledgements

'Resistance Days', 'High Water' and 'The Seaside Cemetery' first appeared in limited editions from The Gallery Press. Thanks are also due to the *Irish Times*, the *Guardian*, the *TLS* and the *London Review of Books*.